IN THE FUNCTION OF EXTERNAL CIRCUMSTANCES

IN THE FUNCTION OF EXTERNAL CIRCUMSTANCES

EDWIN TORRES

NIGHTBOAT BOOKS
Callicoon, NY

book design & graphics: Edwin Torres
chapter drawings and *Liminal Skin* section: Nancy M. Cohen
cover painting & bio photo: Elizabeth Castagna

Grateful acknowledgement is made to the editors of the magazines in which
some of these poems first appeared: *26, 580 Split, Bombay Gin, Chronogram,
Dragon Fire, Fence, Fifi, Heights Of The Marvelous, Longshot, Lungfull, Poets Against
War, The Shore Magazine, St. Elizabeth Street, Torch, Wet, XCP: Cross-Cultural Poetics.*

Segments of this book were produced while in residence with Lower Manhattan
Cultural Council. *Southern Cross* originated at The Sydney Arts Festival and was
finalized in The East Village. *Liminal Skin* was created as a musical collaboration
with Akemi Naito for Composers Collaborative Inc. and re-imagined as a sculpture
& sound installation by Nancy M. Cohen for The Hunterdon Museum Of Art.

Thanks to Stephen and Kazim for your support. Special thanks to Ram Devineni,
Carol Mirakove, Rebecca Wolf, Nancy M. Cohen and Elizabeth Castagna for their
contribution towards the shaping of this book. And to the open beings who filter
through each of our lives affecting an untold capacity for reach and connection.
My heart to Harry, Max, Rubio Jett and . . .

———————————

ISBN: 978-0-9822645-5-3
Cataloging-in-publication data is available from the Library of Congress.

Distributed by University Press of New England
One Court Street
Lebanon, NH 03766
www.upne.com

Nightboat Books
Callicoon, NY
www.nightboat.org

...Elizabeth

"The sensuous
breathing body is
a dynamic,
ever-unfolding
form, more a
process than a
fixed
or
unchanging object."

David Abram
The Spell Of The Sensuous

\/ \/\/\
\/ \/\/\

\/\\/\
\/\/\/

SUNSPOT

WRAPPED UP

shiny in the spine
this gift
what you get from giving

let's change
and keep breathing
what we get from breathing

is that light
or tunnel, can't tell
without landing

this image amazed
by clarity
what embraces clarity

do we ask
what we know
or what we want to hear

the parable chosen
before
the gift

IN LINE WITH WHAT

At odds with what heaven must be.
Sharp angle to my height, a question.

Could that be it? A question?
Here on this momentary point, my view is tiny

to whatever answer waits. There is
a rotating shadow circles my pen.

As I write, and all this surface
below me seems not much for awhile.

Is heaven this solitary? A cave in my brain . . .
if in it, already? What,

one thing more, makes it heaven?
Nothing here, says it.

No one. My pen, I s'pose
is heaven. Easy this question.

What makes what I have
a start?

FOG

mere blank
this boy
this air
mere room
this birth
this fog
mere height
this man
this page
mere wind
this world
this day

THE LEGENDARY MOON ESCAPES

what makes this
be what makes
this —

what's not what's
me what's not
is —

so not is
what is what
is —

what's be
is what is not —
is

MYSTERY PRIZE

        let me
tell you something
about arriving—it only means
you're not
        where you were

SQUARES

ear to diagonal
stretched
body to wall
unstable shift—
shaped

centered
by impression
defined—
by nation
of silent squares

trapped in catch
smiled
by pale refraction
empty sea
circles my home—was it you

eye to level
obscured by revelation
aroused
by nomad's reflection—
holding—what folds in two

TREE

And these hands
uprooted—3 fingers splintered
And these scragged needles
ripped through earth
And this field
captured by violet sound
And this tree
how was it placed to be looked at
And now midnight
And this parade has passed
And that star field
And these fingernails
eleven stars in every cuticle
And this grip
this sky molten solstice
And all these earth-dreamers
wrapped around us
And all the long shadows
like me . . .
placed to be looked at
far from home

ROUGH GRAVITY

was an old friend
old old friend
thought we weren't—that is
old anymore
picked up by 2
planets—perfuct
planets—revolv
ing 'round me—rough
rough gravity—too many
tales in the pedestal
foot—too many friends
who leave me to fall—
need to find
my windowless ground—
coarse
opium—opiate cookie

WE ARE CREATURES OF THE WIND

rotate in similarity
let some past click

what ember flicks when stunned
what burn involves change

what striate shoots across
what sky lets itself be shot

creature breezed by bend
total what leaps

what wind does to leaf
lips to free

EAGLE'S CUBICLE

I remember looking out from high above
not too long ago

floating lazy as I circled my height
immersed in a sky I never owned

the pattern below me as insular as I imagined
while grounded, stuck

in what would never have let me go
if I knew enough—that I'd ever come back

before I was already gone

SARCOPHAGI

luggaged
earthed
mapped
       my corner my dirt my pit
skulled
jawed
veined
       my grass my first my step
rivered
skinned
pulsed
       my cloud my cry my blink
citied
fleshed
watered
       were sky like eye like hand
ghosted
mangled
boned
       my mountain my rot my crypt
hidden
blinded
layered
       intact horizon intacted fracture
opened
framed
dusted
       my window my glass my lens
erased
rubbed
bent

WASN'T BORN TO FOLLOW

this is about starts
working into your layers
how secrets linger
before they reveal

let's revolve around
revolving
wash storms replaced
by seeing

how reflection
positions you
in line
with squint

that burn on the horizon
a reminder
that even speed
needs to start somewhere

SUNSPOT

it is the man
at one with word
that is word

so that
word and no word
are one

and
is
becomes

still, what you do to yourself
is as height as time is—forever reflecting
the spot you stand in

the man at that spot
has found something greater
than the spot he has found

it was a span of time or a year
that I thought I mastered—thought only—through delusion
that illusion is comfort

finding when faced with what's real
that comfort is ally to lethargy—the easiest stone
becomes the heaviest turn

if this be my spot
let it find me whole
desirous of calamity or else its *freeze*

at once humbled and smaller
from what appears to be the only impact—
the scar of what you go through

walking habits will choose best
when to appear
after having *gone through*

and how often
comfort becomes pride—equally dangerous
yet comforting

for it is the standing
that has found the spot
greater

than the spot
that has found
the man

| | | | |
| | | | |

| | | | |
| | | | |

| | | | |
| | | | |

| | | | |
| | | | |

ONE TO ONE

IN THE SPEED OF SLOW

how is the weather and cities, we say, how sky it is
and children, how skin on bones and flesh, we say, here
is a broken man before you, animated with respect

and shared daring, a destiny to deceive what he holds back
as we talk and laugh, if you only knew, we say, that he's broken
in two, and the news and how are you we say, and what's left

is a container for memory and deception, yours and mine
as deceit gathers, underneath the surface of atmosphere, both
yours and mine, where atoms, both of them, position themselves

as they wait for reception, I'm much slower now, we say,
the people around me, transformed by static, my skin
opened to the speed of slow, sun is my partner, we say,

as we graze the ground for fuel, our fingers reach
beyond height, we catch distance in mouthfuls, as everyone
continues at ridiculous speeds, we part the wake, the air behind

fractures in tomorrow appear today, my legs, we say, rubbery
and charged with static, the edge of air reveals itself
my breath, we say, begins again, from childhood to downpour

I could catch bullets if I were that lazy, we say, open raindrops
before they fall, I can taste reflection before its decision, navigate
skin underneath speed, the taste of clouds assumes I've arrived

we say, our ankles warm on asphalt shimmer, we step outside
what's muscle and flesh, the view, an incision from then to wow
my options grow as I slow down, the air I'm in, the one I've left,

my pulse is periphery attached to speed, we say,
my body pulled to the skin of slow

TO HAVE ONCE BEEN AB

We bring past around
to meet future, making past angry
as it compares and notes astonishment
at we and our wants from future,
from what past had. How could that have
made we happy? Just lookit what we want
from future; cute, huh, THAT? Oh lover bum,
sorry for the failed missive, the fired shot
at time, and we, so abnormal see how
it is sick and normal
to be so ab.

THE LAW OF THE APPLE

we convince ourselves of what we need
allowing obstacle a rebirth as reason

the ground cracks our body reacts
adjusting balance with footing, ear canal to cochlea

perspective shifts as focus clarifies, position of neck
to spine merges into planet's gyration

we orbit the occipital orb
the eyeball retracted by obstacle's incision

merged into our head our feet, somehow planted
on our eyes, as ground shakes we adjust our view

our heart follows close behind looking for an orbit
to call its own, gravity tells a story . . .

> . . . has falling helped you see how to stand. will melting away
> cover improve intuition. porous like mine. I want to fall in
> the nothing. find what's there. challenge my something
> with surrounding nothing. maybe the certain. question the
> maybe. enter the sweat of what falls before I catch it. attach
> impulse to tributary. feather away grass from its skin. remind
> each blade of my pores. my static charge of light and dusk.
> magnetize distress. vanish emblems of pointed palmistry.
> paining hull. esperanza savior. salivant sonority. have you
> instincted the instants yet. stepped in line. what is the water
> like when followed unwillingly. when skin is checked
> by the surface of surround. the speed of slow.
> who gets wet in the blade of water that cuts the wake.
> is there friction with a name for blend. do I remove the
> image before it envelops. rescue the outcome before it lands.

GEEK FLESH AMERICA

I am not to be scurried off
dispensed at the end of a longful night

I am not a person
whose charge—unwilled esperanza
lopes about unchanged

I am not to be cut off
from available heart's diffusion—
mainstay of contradictive suck-offs

I am not a blister
charting out the night's adrenaline
longing for incompletion's parity will

I am not for the faint of open skulls
a wretched epic stuck in mythic battle with ego-headed hoopsters
zoot-suited for a roll in the hay with digital bone suck

This lasso craves a neck
bootystuck on hambone wrestlemaniac's yesteryear—
my jumbling yester-yaya song

I am not a yellow dog
in line with feral opportunity
flaked onna mission eeked out against mindloop

I am not a chested wookie blessed by spum
left born right struck
town

Not geek flesh America
skinny fatso redcheek spum cap
brown haze over lazy chest pops

Smoghole landtrap seersucker boy long
weapons not fake names that sound
just like me

SOME NOTES ON PRINCESS DI

Not sure how life is affecting. How someone you never met is affecting. Must have missing part inside. Missing what's missing. To feel any need of affecting. Was a nation inside. Entire nation in my heart. For former lover's love. How affecting. That. Life is lovers' love and all of lovers' life is time for lovers' of.

A former one. Who once traveled this nation. Entire nation inside me. Was signing me. Movements in air of handtalking. Was his hand talking. I took this as a sign. That I was not so easy to see. So hard to control. Was I. Merely chaoticized wind sprint. In my palm. Was outstretched missile.

My hand when I look at I see. My former lover's love. This was all right to spend time on. Because. I wasn't there anyway. This that I say. All happened before I knew. My former love had I. Nothing to do with it. My hand I mean. Looking. Like his. Was I. Time controlled. But out of. How affecting was I.

To someone I haven't met yet. French horn comes in. Slow and walrus-like. A penguin on television. A fairy-blue one. Swims out all day. Comes back. Stuffed with dinner. Gather the hordes. To watch the arrival. Concrete seats built into the beach. A collection of watchers waiting. For little fairy penguin. To come home. Ten bucks a seat.

everybody's looking—   just want to get home—   and everybody's looking—

This. Was little sea bird talking. Little blue one drenched with ocean. Such a flightless little back. Was his trouble. To be the loner with a burrow. Such a song of alone. Was mine too but. No ones's looking at me. When I get home. My beach is unpopular. There is no attraction. No seats to rent. No one follows.

When I go home. I put my keys in. No one is there. Before my love I mean.
No one was watching. Was just time. Before. When I was there. Alone.
To pass until. Time gets tired of being passed through. Time wakes up to you.
Tells you not to pass me through. Says: Make sure. You know. Of me so.
You. Make sure. You know. Of you. At 10 bucks a seat.

What this has to do with fairy blue. I was reminder to former love of love.
Because. I was as free as former lover's love. This was made clear to me.
At the end after the end. Of our love together. This was made clear.

More than my hands. I was more than I was. To former love. All time. All
our time together. Had been. Me. Inside shell. Of passed away love.
Someone's life was I made to be. Unknown to me. Until the end. At the end.
Who. I didn't know. Would never meet. Like nation's love. Her nation's love.
For fairy princess.

Avoiding everyone. Who wants to see. How she. Goes home. Her nation
chasing her. Watching her go home. How could he pass away. Leave her.
For me. Before she. Could go home. Little fairy penguin. Such a flightless little
home. The shore. Is where they wait for you. The shore. Is what they watch.

MONDAY UNTITLED

but I am left alone when I sink
and you
are there but I don't see

here I have split off
into two
meaning harm meant good

and though I say I let you
we both know this reliquary of good faith
remains untitled

---

we're almost
in each other's hands now

my moment here
a tendon stretched out of reach

I thought this would become something
instead, my tone is light

as a wall at once
seperating and protecting

I was wondering who did that
and who put that
and that's amazing
right right you say

I only name them
once they belong to someone
until then, I leave them
surprised

having a good time
how are you and
who's happy today huh who's
happy

CHIARASCURO

This fire I smell
prophetic air—uncharged
am I still
in this shadow I bought as a child?

I thought its warranty expired
replaced in my *adult* life—
is this adult?
To say *I should have*
and live in hindsight?

This air—
surrounding sirens
and devastation—my twin nightbirds.
Smoked like any port city, New York
is a meandering glitter.

How many times
can I claim
my hometown before the mirrored reflection
resembles the fire I smell?
The adult I am.

Hiding in my age—no moon
behind smoke, only tidal shift of
noise and height.

My hometown lets me scale
to fall the hardest climb.
Can I take this to heart
by turning an ear
to night's soliloquoy of freedom?

Uncharged—this fired air
at once smoked
and loved.

HOW TO SOAK YOUR FEET WHEN THEY'RE COLD

Almost married, my tepid arrangement with supposed singularity has left me
bereft of any machoneering impulse to abide by the rhythm of nuyoricua and give
in to my tepid results—that I am no longer a handsome dud—I mean dude—
but an unavailable monster. A good catch for all women to cherish in this time
of goody-goodness. Here lies the rascal who won't commit, step right up and kiss
this mug! Oh, it is all too sad.

I am one who has keys to his bachelor pad, but there is no bachelor pad like this
one. I have a studio on the second floor, at the end of the block—is a dream I had
of having this ownership. What I had was the dream, not the apartment. What a
rush this is now, ten years later. How time decides to catch you when you're up
for it, not when you want it.

I have keys to this second floor paradise. The neighbors *understand* my situation,
agree with my solution, *abstain* from contact. I arrive periodically to get my mail,
feed my cats. I am leading a double life, a bigamist of opportunity—not humans,
not wives. I have just one wife—or is that my honeymoon haze, my newlywed lie?

Did I tell you I thought this was a dream? This terror of two lives, agreeably
penchant for timeless temerity, the ten-year itch awakened by wood-bugs, crawl-
ing crustaceans on a wood-burning vacation imported by solitude, who dare me
to revisit my dream? *"And I will off your previousness with charmless stoppability,
reaped in the sophomoric tremors of the devilishly inclined . . ."* Huh? Yeah! That's
what I mean—that I was checking my mail for one month at my old apartment
while married in my new one.

The cats would be moved in time, but first a honeymoon was in order, and then a
change of address—or was that the dream part? How could anyone leave animals

in a summer wait while deciding how to lose their crutches, how to find the adultness of coupledom, how to gain supposed wisdom while maintaining ferocious municipality, independence, or solitary fortune? I had trouble adapting to empowerment. Give me a moment and I'll remind you why this gut check is such a punch. Now, ten years later.

Imagine thinking you thought something, and all your years that thing you thought was not a question, never doubted. All your years you had done that *thing*, a memory safely preserved—for good or bad—you'd done that thing, you'd live on and do it, you'd go and be. The manners of your action, everything in your muscle memory, the entire ritual of this action existed without question—as breath on skin.

The years encapsulate your whim and seconds. Time ensures your escape when one day you close your eyes briefly. You blink like the millions of blinks you've had, the eyelid down, then up quick, a gulp of water for seeing. After that blink you awaken a memory, or is it a thought, or is it a question—can all three happen at the same time? You attach a realization to the moment after that blink. You attach an entire history to the seconds attached to that momentary sartori, that awakening, the emblazoned passage of seasons pretended by time to be memory. What if you came out of that blink and questioned a ten-year memory aroused by fear and predilection?

The important facts are not important. The decided notions are undecided. What counts is the fact that your brain could do this to you. Your own mind could trick you into this thievery. What if what remained instilled by virtue of respect amidst treason was a lone tremor implicit in its being? A final instinct created by time's own question to you and your distant history. What if the reason for your sudden groundlessness was a mere turn at the space you've been handed?

Stilled by the ravage of decision, mind and time will pair up for a brave front— the allies flaming when least terrified. What is my head giving me so that this change can happen with comfort? I haven't received any clarity, any chance for double duty in all this, so I remain in the smack of what I woke up in—that what had mattered to me, in the passage of mattering that happens over a lifetime, when what you've remembered is a comfort, a disciple or discipline of a warrior or worry, the place as true to you as breath in the time of its skin—had been nothing but a blink.

That your brain could do this to you, could choose the treachery of what I swore was . . . I'm telling you, I had the key to both apartments, I got the mail, I swore I did. I remember the cats, waiting everyday, I had two lives, not wanting to give up either, the neighbors across the street, the store below that kept changing owners, the house at the end of the block. But there is no house, no picket fence with friendly mailman, I see that now, it was never there, this is the East Village!

Then why is this all so clear to me? In one blink, how could this entire scenario set root, only to be exposed? How could I have looked forward to those steps, the low light in my first apartment, long orange shadows from the sun, my cats, my bed that I never slept in, the mail . . . I swore I got the mail.

MONDAY AFTERNOON

I

see i thought this should be
as easy to get into as it was
to start

us not having done it
for such a long time, i was concerned
with making it as smooth as i remembered it

how that first move
is followed by such a slow second
almost rainy but nicer

i never used to say *nice*
it's such a sign of weakness
you know uncommitted, stuck between *great* and *blah*

i'm falling again and you
are momentary in your waking
is this what it was we were *missng*

the second i replaces the s, i
m misspelling this memory
the right music reminds me how smooth we were

or nice I could say
quiet guitar fills the point between nice
and us, the pavement appears with rain-soaked accents

sybillant saxophonic symmetry
jarred awake from years of lunacy
i see you asleep

our hands start
now, what was it
kept us still so long

II

maybe this is a series
a collection of fingers on a handout
the grey day that takes no grey
but gives grey a day to think

they see us reach the door
simultaneous from a city of errands
we happen to get home at the same time
i know you we both say

you are today what i
dreamed about before i knew you
it took this long
in both our lives for that to happen

but is that what this is about
how i continue to resist telling you
about your beauty because that
would make you more beautiful

and i don't know that i could stand
such beauty being sad
because *that* is what this is about
how in the eyes of the beholder

such beauty is rain but in the eyes
of beauty such rain is just rain
and if i could take just rain
and make it beauty for you

if you could see what i see
is when i wonder about translation
how to place beauty in what i see
just because i see

how it is that sadness brings me
to a place without walls
and so a place where my *see*
is as wide as it is deep

when i didn't know you
we were both waiting
then i dreamed i saw you
i know you we both said

the image before us
unformed
as love is unborn
before us

III

but sometimes
there is only an idea
of what i want you to be
with an idea
of what i am

or is this
what i see
where i want you
to see
sometimes

see
i may need you
to be who you are
for me
when i need you to

but don't think
i'm needing you
just
for the needing
of what you are

or is that the idea
of what you had
when
all you had
was me

see us
there
in
each other
with all we see

that's where i stand
with what we have
in having this us
what we see as us
is having it all

here
let's say there's
no need no
want maybe now
i see

ONE BY ONE

Who tricks who? After I show you my bruise, you still seem surprised
by my skin. After we lie on each other's tummies, you burp out silent air
and shake me from a dream, with your belly as my pillow.

I was surrounded by a circle of legs. Each ankle, draped with my favorite pair
of your panties. Each leg standing solo, no body attached yet
very much alive and perfect, as tall as I was. One by one, I was to begin

behind each knee and start my tongue. What direction I went in
depended on whatever a giant loudspeaker hanging overhead would yell out.
The atmosphere was electric with sex, yet brutal, in a work-for-hire kinda way.

I was lying over you, our bodies intertwined. One long stroke
would follow a few short ones. As we stared into our eyes my hands
were somehow holding your long back. We were suspended

over a blanket as large as a room. I started to say something,
your hand covered my mouth, I put my hand on yours to move it away
and lost my grip. You plummeted.

I saw your naked body falling away from me, your hair wild,
a black parachute with silver streaks. Your hips and perfect ass,
a mannequin out of my reach. You landed on the blanket as I was

burped awake by your belly.

> There is no length attached to our consumption
> my hunger, a constant parasite
> for what's just out of reach.
>
> There is no curve for the name of our bodies
> inside you, my hands are just now
> in touch with this fall.

OURS IS LENT BY HOURS' RELENT

your flood carressed me
     made me open my heart
your flood carressed me
     made me open my heart   your flood
         surrounded my heart
            made me open you did
         flood me you did
I dropped what I had
     made it a terrible deal
dropped what I did
     made a terrible deal   I opened what I had
         made me up to a terrible deal
            I dropped what I opened
         my heart a terrible deal
your garden gave me biscuits
     a blonde brownie in summer
your garden gave me sunshine
     a summer dirt deal   I opened what I gave you
         a summer of my heart
            this window I look out on
         as open as the wind
this window I look out to
     as garden as the wind
         as dropped as what I dealt
            surrounded by my heart
         a flying height of embers
     a rolling house of doubt
a lying flame undone   my heart an open summit
         a flood for what you did
            my heart an open summit
         a flood for what you did

DO NOT BE SWAYED BY EXTERNAL CIRCUMSTANCES

-what would happen if you let the ground support you
-yeah, but it's supporting you too

the ocean arrives in one hour, no edge where we are
no ground underfoot, no seaweed above, no distance too raw
we walk the ocean floor, swept by vacant surf, its red soil
filled with seabirds dining on fresh catch, newly exposed
by settled horizon—what would happen, if there were no edge
to ocean or land, our feet sinking in every step

the tide is coming, I say, *we need to leave the ocean floor*
grassy field runs along rock shore, curved cove
outlines seaspray roar, *the water's coming,* I say again
while pointing, we're closer to shore's edge straight ahead
than behind, means going through mud marsh, no problem
we think, only slippery not deep, we thought

ladybug landed on your head, *look what I found,* you said
transporting ladybug to hand-carriage, *look mrs. ladybug we're going on a trip*
this is pretty special isn't it look where we're going
legs travel fast, I follow smaller feet, my sandals mud-caked, still,
forward progress being made, until undertide softens ground
ankle deep, legs stuck, mud engulfed, can't lift

wait for me you should follow my feet
they're bigger than yours, I yelled and caught up,
tide, still an hour away by sight, underneath by inches
pleasant breeze disguises afternoon sun
wearing demon cloak, caught up, *now you follow me,* I say
sandals sinking, fear roots the steady pulse, don't let on, forge ahead

smaller feet follow mine, towel in one hand, mrs. ladybug in the other
follow the leader, until trapped by mud, *I can't move,* you scream
I'm scared, far ahead I yell, *okay just breathe and wait,* I backtrack
to your rescue, until I can't move, ankles lost, solidified with every
attempt to lift . . . stop, think quick . . . *if foot is trapped remove foot . . .*
I reach down, remove sandals, fighting engorged mud disguised as ground

bare feet slip through, dirt hands hold sandals the size of boulders
by their caked leather tongues, as if I've caught death-mud
by its feelers, *take off your shoes I did it and I can move now*
take off your shoes, I repeat, seems as if tide is roaring in
although still a football field away, underneath, it's real, we're trapped
take off your shoes, I scream, my feet sinking with every shiver

at this point mrs. ladybug remembers her wings, calibrates her chances
and takes a hike, holding shoes in hand, we look ahead, we look behind
thinking to retrace steps, not thinking those steps are gone by now, swallowed
below a million snails, submerged on ocean floor, newly revealed
like breath bubbles at low tide, red mud chugs halfway up limbs,
this chapter was not in the guide books, backpack, towels, camera

all non-adventure conventions, held high above, as if we were waist deep
not ankle shins, external circumstance lurking beneath,
when you're pulled by something unexpected, what you know
gets replaced by what you feel, and the earth you thought you knew
is unwoven by the elemental might out of your grasp, fear finds its comfort
placid blue sky bears witness, to two travelers sinking

this can't be happening, in the eternity of false seconds given to last riters
we calculate three choices in the afternoon sun . . . one, retreat back
to point of origin, four times distance of shore ahead . . . two, walk through
equally distant unproven swamp on the left asking water spirit, would curved
marsh grass as tall as we are imply steady ground, long skinny ladders wait
along coast, like fingers grasping rocky cliffs, reaching up to homeowners
who know better . . . or three, maintain our path and focus

in a burst, survival and breath kick in, we bolt
straight ahead, our road clear, no turning back, feet squirm
through a million snail shells, outracing the enveloping ground
breath steady, my feet following yours, moving fast, mud has no time to trap
invisible tide reaches underneath, bastard mud finds a ditch, in we go
up to our knees, progress stops

wait for me, you yell, *hurry I'm really sinking*
I catch up to you, *hold my hand here pull up*
you were beautiful with your black mane
caught by ocean's current, the sweep of our bodies
against low tide, submerged in red clay
water filled our lungs, the mighty currents liplocked on ours

we were holding hands under the rising lift
my edge, the skin of our separation, the boundary we touch
at every morning's length, follow my feet
bigger than yours, my lead following yours, wait for that time we fell
ten years ago, into the brook, we dropped two daisies
yours swirled ahead of mine, found a rock, and waited

IN EACH LOOK OUR YEARS

that's it
that I walked into the cafe
and in the noise and crowd
we met

and that I saw
what it was I'd been
in what it was
I saw

that in our skin
in the decade of our skin
is what began
before we knew

and that time before
with this time now
is nothing
waiting to start again

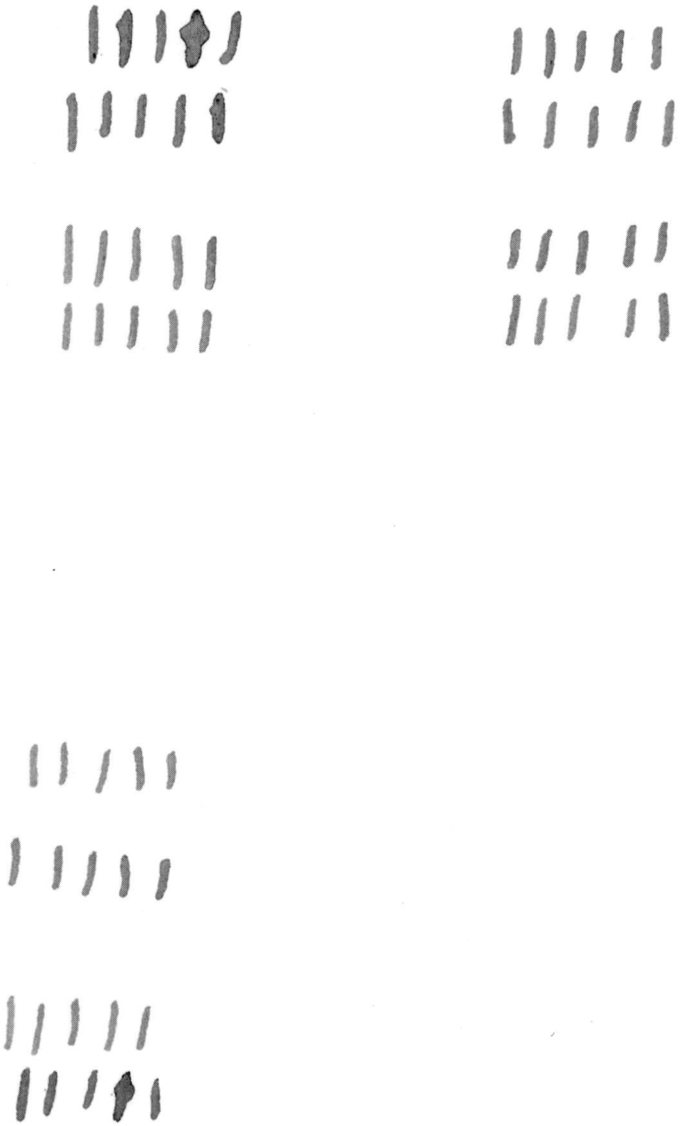

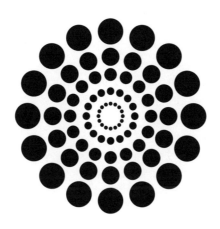

UNDERNEATH THE SOUTHERN CROSS

A Diary Of A Journey

* * * *

WORD PUZZLES
CROSSWORD POEMS
POEZZELLES
PUZZ-EL-EMS
POZZLES
PEMMELLS
POMM-ELL-EPPELLS
PUMMELS
WORD PUMMELS
distinct BLAMS!
come about POUP!
infusing the safety of word puzzles
PASSELS, PIZZLES and PIPS
into the deity ever
y-EV
day-ITTY BLANCHE
MALIGNANCHE
AVALIGNANCHE
BALANCHE

IN-compre-HANCHE
FREE-RANCH
take a
CHANCH wit' me . . .
take a word pummel
decisive sculptor
scalped to incise the word open
to jamble pamp the screwer by the bay
the day . . .
THED-AY
THA-TADA!
TA DA! TA DA!
TA DA! TA DA!
GABBA-RA!
GRABBA!

GRAB-A-HA!
RABA-HO!
NAVAJO!
AMMA-NO-WAY
gonna GRABBA dat!
SISOR-
CISOR-IN
CASE you-IN
CASE-a-CISOR
YOU - in CISE a
inside-A-MASE
IN-A-MASE a SUNDAYS
a SIDE 'a ME . . . comes out
a side of spired and steepled chances
a church I can believe in

        *   *   *   *

in the rafters of a stained-glass ceiling
in the catacombs of an incomplete blunder—the evening sky
tries to find me
constricting its scaffold around me—the inconsolable sky
tries to fool me

I wait—to please—
but I know where I want illumination and chance
is a far shadow from here
a starlit apology shimmering its cross

a church with white wings
that fall when they flap—at the core
with a cloud at my waist my legs
fall off
when I walk in this kind of night

      I don't applaud my blunders often
      but this one seems to warrant a standing ovation

the scaffolding
rises in my afternoon now
barely shadows itself
across my sunset frame
my stained glass—wide as blue sky

as evening is an empty blunder
waiting to please

        *   *   *   *

        Pornographic nurse
        I love our chest . . . how are we
        doing today, can we ramp it up a bit?
        Hanky in the mornin'

        *   *   *   *

coffee bar in Melbourne
Fitzroy, East Village of Australia
waiter has green glasses of metal he got in France
wonders where my glasses' country is from
Korean, I think, in a five-dollar frenzy
American, I say, the latte is made—two big photo prints
onna wall here on Brunswick Street, dark prints beauty prince
charming is our bloke of a waiter—handsome oldie, bigger than ever
sits outside our window, black fedora onna graybeard face
summer heat knows his coat, he must
waddle into the 90's by his crawl—lookit this man Oh he's so handsome
some old men are downright cute, but this one
has the outback scribbled into his wrinks, he sits, I write
look up, he's gone—on to Brunswick Street
like we, after our fruity latte and passionfruit expressionless
like the folke at home we pass every day on Bleecker
and Christopher, who we say are lazy waste-aways
like we, here—on holiday—streaming sun sits betweening
legs and kneesing sun 'etween our bees

* * * *

rising up to the race of another rip
                TONGUELASH   EYEBLINK
MANBOY   KNEEHIGH
                MECHANISMO   MACHISMO
MACHINALIA   MECHISMUS
                ole sol you know all and make sure I know it

                constantly under your flesh
so savage your knifed existy plane—
                tell me how I matter
how I gain your trust at every mistake—
                how the platform I'm on
is slowly chiseled to reveal
                shadows and fear—
the shoulders I use for a better view

* * * *

Here I am, masked by a mystic forest under a canopy of translucent palms
Where lightcurve's might hides from six-foot sunflowers dazed by belonging
Swallowed by flutterdarts of cover and crook
Hunched by a lifetime stripped of darkskullery
Where banyan trees breathe easy over the copper-winged landflappers
Who burrow into soft volcanic rolls and rise in shadow's crashing mystery
Paintsinging long hours across gardens of sunbrown skin
Scrawn on angels out of wedlock
With eyes that smile deep into the banyan trees
Who host the parasite seed
That roots through whatever branch gets in the way
Where I can dunk my sins in an ocean of rainbows
So I can breathe easy as trees
Sightless as a nothing bird
Searching for land

* * * *

Here I am, squeezed
on a "caff" on the side streets
of a "happ" in a 'nother "sect"
of the world

Bohemian is a catchphrase
thrown out by No-hemians
everything's designed "just so," there ain't no rawness
Feel the sprint of early morning showers
gone but here, not forgotten—incline to my latte
on a foreign alley, a sidestreet hotspot

I am exotic against these people
against the angular sun gods
I am merely a dark shoot
rifle shot darkman, glowing hard
carbon hard ebonite light
M'aura Maori
I have indigenous blood
though I'm from the streets of a city
my blood runs sideways
underneath the Southern Cross

My face turns slightly
toward the red skies at day's end
My face turns toward the feel
of a goodbye sun
Blood of Boricua
Skin of New York
Moricua, Bori,
Baoricua, amor

* * * *

servant for tragedy
        {engine erratta}
errant disguster
        {elegia makker}
chakked irronio
        {rigored immorta}
circular kara-meo
        {celibate noser}
facial treeshaver
        {buttonfly swigger}
crazed imposs-ohm

I am now playing with your catch
and will I be your match, c'mon
strike me—SPLATCH
again, the box—*{alga zebow}*

*   *   *   *

off to swim, in the great cataclysm
of the orgy-fused constant

*   *   *   *

what passion fills in for gimmick
balance of heart and intellect, rebalances no thinking

quiet experiential methodpulse
what scrams about, searching glare of shiner eyes

burnt when escaped by ocean weight
what sweeped little wings chirped out young fuzzy night

specks inter-camera, inter-flash avoidance
sightless nature, undrunk savage

flash of blind shiner man
creeps along without a blinkstone

what soaked up windswept rock
cries every night for setting sun's despair

reckless rock charred by oceanic charcoal
ebonitely pavement, nominated for easiest hire

easiest path toward drowning burn
what darling fire

* * * *

Dear David,

We're on a South Pacific island
400 miles away from Australia—a million miles
away from everywhere
We'll have spoken before you read this
so I'll only write sunshine bits and
reef lowisms particular to my state of mind
at this wave—Blue is Green only between
your toes, when under 2 feet of
ocean, feet are a pattern migrating
across darks left by ripples of breeze
The green of this isla
is a massage across time, and she knows
only mountains until she grows home—I am now
a dark passage-flip, grainy pours and blue ... which was green
when she came from the ocean

* * * *

- *fuel fyres the orange seam . . . in colors we can only hear . . . up here thrown into the velvet*

- *every catch . . . a solid planet, smart wink of fyre . . . sky was owner when coral was finder*

- *my face under my mask . . . scuba dives below slumber . . . with stolen air snorkel the cloud reefs*

- *under the I . . . balance to find . . . glass chariot skin pressed by temple*

- *features find ocean . . . tickling the outreach . . . the snarly shapes that scare me*

  - *in the little holes of coral*
  - *are the little fish that call me*
  - *in the little city below me*
  - *are the little people waiting*

  * * * *

  woven world—gigantic ball
  to step over, to stroke your belly—unmasked
  as a planet exposed
  a starfish to place starts on

  unhyphenated conch shell
  basking to celebrate begins—
  as a wave mates along the shore
  in thunderous carpety lace of sound bump

  place a start where it wants
  then leave it—to start again
  as a baby ball knows to fold
  underneath gigantic steps

* * * *

Tried to catch you I did
Holding my ears out
         I ran
         Offering the waves a sacrifice
               Extending my range
               Like I thought I could—like . . .

     To hear might so mighty
     You close your eyes
     You focus on a pinpoint
     You take yourself to the roar under sand . . . *you*
           . . . with me now?
     You scale infinity as my arms could only be and me
     Stuck on earth with only one note
           . . . your breath caught you asleep and your snore
           . . . was this poem I let myself be swallowed in

O KareKare
Will I ever see you again
Running your long throat
Down your molten shore
A constant roar
An engine
Blasted open
Like sound under sand
Waiting to catch you
With ears stretched out
Like drowning
With ears stretched out stuck here
Incapably yours
          . . . if I stand still I can hold you
          . . . will you ever be with me again
          . . . or do you know something I don't

* * * *

Through the flying machines
she stands with me, looking out over the waters
it's the same land we're on . . . just a little
further . . . that's all. Plumed forest creature, unleashed
for a night through the flying machines.

* * * *

I fell & then I stretched
& then your hand & then
I fell

* * * *

you promised wonder
in a new position—
in the base of spine calma
I was a skinny light
in a blown out black night—my vicious
was a screaming road
screaming red skull
crying a mating yell

we were nocturne by new moon
your bicycle had a rope
holding the rear rim—
I was a *whirrrr* zinging in the dark
old moon remained hidden
by yesteryear's memory of the same yell—vicious lectern
laughter to wild vectum *verrs* &
merry at these scrawny bones holding still

* * * *

Every downtown has a city does every city have..

Do you read your own..
                          ..take

                    ..throw
Does your throat pick up every scratch when you hear the boring..
                    ..finish

                                        ..tongue
Would you let yourself be used in someone's..
                                              ..too easy

                              ..verb
Could you stand to swim in saliva if your strokes were versed in...
                                              ..world

                        ..sleep
Do you scuba-dive below slumber when tomorrow steals your..
          ..girl

                              ..stress
Could you place forgiveness shadows on shoulders of..
                    ..work

Does it matter when you..

Wanna boy or a.. (wanna boil a curl)

          *   *   *   *

Fanny-Be Buzzrock
Jeepa Meanie Chola-Roll

          *   *   *   *

forever sound in the nitely swim
forever gone to pen the mighty glares
dropped — a free pass to libertine vests
painted by our newfound bankruptcy

* * * *

Runamuck & SOS
Cartaround & Showoff the
Un - Usual   an - I - mal
I am bad   *and*
I am malo   y   I soy   *and*
And I if AM I   *and*
I soy   un muy mal   y low   *and*
Y   *and* ...   y   *yo* ...   we go
Y both soy   when I was ... am I
Was an I baddo *O no* ... soy
Malo soy masque   co - ro - RAddo
O - RA - o   red *death*
Un red   *bad* red
For a bad   *and*
I was   red *death*
Con - strict - ted   red *bad*
Strang - gelled   red *mal*
an AN - I - MAL   of   de - *CEPT* - tion
un - *USUAL*   an - I - mal
Me layo son - tuno con
Paranja zibrana ... o - tra vez y
Charada ... parada - Stop me - *if you've heard this before*

· * * * *

Pubic sand knee-high, 7 morning AM
No cloud on Gower Mountain
Moon is ghost
For last night skilly
Wanderer facing bravados
Too wimpy for night

Me-island, what island
Is that? It's not on the map!
Me-Island! with rising
Uncertain tyranny and falsing
Ice-faces . . . cliffs you could dream off
Greens of audio
Filamental screams, where the
Nothing Birds come to
Clumsy landings and right
Conclusions, water massages
With morning . . . I am nothing
On Me-Island

HORIZON IS INTERRUPTED BY REEF:

    excuse me!   excuse me!   excuse me!

Meshed Light Retina
Return to Turn
Deep Light Shadow Cover
Over to Other
Overlight
I'm a gentle stroke over your
morning hips—why lips? not ships?
I'm a slow gain on your
morning skin, grain tight
as delirium castles—anchor
to where I was swinging

    * * * *

to where I was—
and back—and to and I was
and to and back—and this
was my father
very small on ground
everything—very small
back—and up where I could see

more than I was supposed to
where I could see that my father
was—very small
            than you got bigger—
than you got small—
            than bigger—
than smaller—stop don"t do that
            I shouldn't see you smaller than me . . .

very big on ground
when he stood over me and
proud of me and I—son of a Torres
and I would carry on—and did you know
I would be so skinny . . . Pop? just like you
turning to the low sun and losing
a shadow for every one gained
as shadow underwater as I am
overground—pushed on a swing
"Look at my son, don't cry,
don't be a silly boy, they're all looking,
see, look at my son," higher than
the world I was—higher than the screams
of a little boy—higher and higher—
"Look at my son!"

and I was to see that I would
never see who you were—up here
where you pushed me to I saw you
not as you were—but as I saw you

a small man on the ground
letting something else go

                *   *   *   *

teiveivei—*birdy gotta birdy-bo*
teiveivei—*witta big gabba-bitty-bo*
teiveivei—*birdy boppa lip-alongo*
teiveivei—*gotta birdy singa-songo*
teiveivei—*witta wings 'at go-a-low*
teiveivei—*by birdy's in the sky-o*
teiveivei—*eeyai-yai yitty-yo*
teiveivei—*birdy sings a hiya-ho*
teiveivei—*witta wings 'at cover-o*
teiveivei—*cover uppa-luppa worldo*
teiveivei—*witta wings 'at say, hallo*
teiveivei—*issa love a-love-I-know*
teiveivei—*issa lova-lova-lei-yo*
teiveivei—*birdy gogo birdy-yo*
teiveivei—*say hiya birdy bro*
teiveivei—*say whya high below*
teiveivei—*issa lova-lova-my-yo*
teiveivei—*issa love-I-love, hallo world*

*   *   *   *

boy walks into ocean
sliced by ocean
to each corner
was tied each foot
standing
in ripped current each year
skyed by age

to each ocean
was skyed
each walk was each step
another wave
as sky sliced over boy
was ocean
ripped over wave

Dear Gary & Pat,

*We're here, in anticipatory holding pattern, with most nervous host ever, sitting
at his home after arriving from airport. On airline shuttle, met a Brit who'd seen
me on Amsterdam television (hyper-child of globetrotting rickety-slickster)
(circular kara-meo from a few pages ago). It's 9:30pm, just him no wife, in the living
room, not used to small talk, social pants of the family, hung out to dry. No patience
for us young hoopersnappers. Leg shakes at every turn of the head, cuts you off
before you finish, provoking any story into its end. Let's move locale, he suggests.
Let's, we say! Shy artist, shows us his studio, comes to life, wine flows. He drives us
to our flat, apartment for visiting guests provided by university. We are thankful
for this moment, traveling as exotic out-of-towners, connected to lineage of writers
and do-ers by unspoken eccentrics, with rare generosity. Flat has stench of rotting
staying power left by previous visitor. Host apologizes, shows us lights and sheets,
gives us contact info, bids good cheer, we thank him, he leaves. Tiny flat has inclined
ceiling, like living in attic, or French movie. Dresser drawer and kitchen both in nook,
under low angle, sustenance and clothing, to get to them, we continually bump our
heads, adapting to incline at place of most importance. We keep count of each bump
on each head, but lose track (who is the Vicar of Dibbey). The next day we call our
contact, English professor at university, delighted to hear from us, has heard all
about the Café, says the group is its leading light. Afterwards, we embellish concept,
how, upon first meeting, I should show up wearing shorts, Miami Beach sunnies and
a lantern around my neck, reciting, "Mary had a little lamb . . . where's my grant!"
And yes, you had to be there.*

* * * *

to be considered *exotic* . . . you need to travel away from home . . . they say
> **movement away from established order**
at home you're considered *different* . . . but somewhere else . . . they say
+ placement of object
where home is considered *exotic* . . . is where you are considered *exotic* . . . they say
= (im)posture

* * * *

i thought the same chair i sat on
was sitting on a shadow of a crawl
that misplaced itself as i sat on it
while moving as a chair without arms is
what i stayed on until a missile's race saw
what i thought was a nation of seats sitting
on its copy and this coffee cup i've seen it before
tall grandé was small once but my hand was holding
something empty something with no purpose or coffee
as things in this room begin to replace themselves i begin
to stay the same ikea put me together my age is my instructions
as the air around me starts to change my arms get used my voice
is on speed dial i don't answer the phone anymore inside the
ringing machine is someone with my voice explaining that
i'm not "available" now i'm trying to leave this hole by
crawling through the mouth it stole copied by people
who copy people but me and this hole wore each other
one time and now we won't wear anything else
familiarity being my love jones i can get away
wearing anything including nothing since i have
the build for it and no one sees me wearing my
nothing every hole wants to wear me i am an
easy drape very seasonal this being the season for extra wear-nots

　　　*　*　*　*

　　　How attitudinal . . .
　　　GOITER-AEDINAL . . .
　　　ADENOIDAL VIRTUE . . .
　　　GET A BOURBONAL . . .
　　　ANDROGYNING and DRY
　　　UP THE GENDER!
　　　ABORIDNY . . .
　　　GORINAL . . .
　　　GOGO! RIGINAL . . .
　　　AGOBBISSNESS . . .
　　　BLOBLO SINUS . . .

Caught being looked at as an out-er, a real
one-off-the-beat-n-pay-dirt.
Indigenous mooncloth is backdrop for a well-lit bartender
praying in the glow of mucho-nada.

All the scenesters are hipping up
to the blonde wig meshbar downstairs.
DJ sits *with* the people, absorbing
recommends and soundsins for the young and the notso.

Melting candles line up for new disaster along the bar.
Ancient siren is ocean glow, rusted beaners
in tapestry ceilings, swimming in the dark . . .
while a drink drowns my fill.

Egg-crate ladidas, well-tanned and empty.
Screwdrivers without a kick. Out-of-timer, stands out
'cuz of the black we wear—the void—we wear nothing
as best as nothing can be worn!

Drip a shoulder to cry on as night as I.

                *   *   *   *

        I'm as hungry as you are sweetheart, but right now sleep is important
        the bread is round in a brown paper bag
        the cheese is a zodiac sign on a table of superstars, the knife lies in wait

        with determination rooted in the face
        a land carves out what others want from you, darling,
        shapes of expectation are expert dancers with the back of the sun

        determined to tease and intrigue
        as they dip into their turns while you explain how the grey
        is only momentary sky how that avocado is only momentary softness

before indigestion floats
there
laid out on a starfield

is a formation of planets waiting to be consumed, sweetheart . . .
I know we didn't have anything but it's late, and at this hour
I think sleep is more important

*   *   *   *

why does world want to be America
                        American TV hubblescopes
            into faraway living rooms
exotics exoticize into American jeans
                              hybrid escapades
                delovely floras and farantinas
pharacide into American four-eyes
            winking into deadeye sunhead
                        why take American sunhead
into shiney Mister Blind Head
                flapping right behinder, kindly
            take my eyes away ole sunhead
                        don't want your worries
when sky's away I know to play
                why faraways be ice flow inversion
            thrown into blue by white limbo info lazlo nympho
                        —those ones wrecked in two are strato nimbo—
not Americo this sky ain't
                today's too young to represent
            yesterday's young, same nubile limbs
                        same trips across rips, same year
            different skips

*   *   *

agent paralysis
comes to me in my sleep
exploiting one byway
for another

*   *   *   *

she impales herself on sorry
lets it wash over her tangle
molded in the furrows
of her every changing sky
what flavor you gonna try
what howl surrounds your lips
take a step onto the ball—take it

and bring your first book
the one with your innocent writings
take your time
with its ramblings—how can I tell you
what you're doing is painful
when the pain
is what you're doing it for—
how expert is it, to be in command

of what you don't know can hurt you—
she makes me
say things like that
like I know
where these words could go
as misguided
as I'll ever be

*   *   *   *

a dream explodes   *& in that explosion*   *a dream*

*   *   *   *

the mountain had no cloud

until the sun made it bright

when cloud saw that mountain was so pretty, cloud came

mountain not moving

lets cloud play

cloud has no home, only home is sky

sky has home on mountain

sky rests on mountain

who lets cloud play on mountain

sun makes sky bright

when cloud sees how pretty sky is

cloud plays in sky

mountain watches, cloud moves, sky changes

sun brights

*   *   *   *

my arm is tired
my arm
has been writing a lot lately—*in the end*
I'm alone but I own what I send—that's good
my arm says, so it writes it down
it keeps going, inside my right-ing forearm
there is a lag, creeping inside, a tingle of fatigue
that dances, with the horses inside my arms

the horses I was told were there—running, like smoke
through my body, like a quirl giving waves
an undulating forecast, a smoky dandelion
a pretty pretty face, my face
was pretty sunshine, petals circled my eyes
receded into my temples, was hearing . . .
to stretch my neck so the horses could have room
to roam, to gallop unleashed
to gather the hurl of smoke, gaining on me
on my dandelion face—I tried
moving my legs, but they were now tree trunks
rooted on the earth, on this ground I
thought I knew, my feet
had eyes on their soles and these eyes
would kiss the ground every time I tried to move
the horses had reached my head now
and my neck had a leak in it
out of which . . . a story appeared:

*   *   *   *

in the flightless incomplete
in the sense of ovary-fory-invacation
invocations of voices sailing past the metric sea-spoon
lite conditions, scattered distractions & changing mental
levels too loud for interruptions of a past skatbone
headwinds on a playground of incomplete

wrangled of neckhang & drooped valley I am
fern-strong for a crazed walk a steady migrate
I cross myself with, let me
sit by the side of my flyers' goodnight and
drink by the elbow the lasting lemon-eyes, let me
walk these borrowed heights that constantly fail me

worries for no one, far . . . I've supposed, once again
for a throwing spoon a shape snailed
in the couries, I was pouring through your
outstretched hands your fingers were the rivers
I raced against—blue, your arms were the distance
I placed myself—green, I patterned my shores

after moments like you, I could fly overever
but here I stay fading distance . . . how colors pale
in a mile-away glance—I'm ready . . . but what I was here for
was not ready, or all was I—here, for an all or not
as I was, and all was I—for a ready to be, or not . . . call me
or come—however you choose, take me to where I can

fall through your fingers again, hear me to where I can
gouge the earth-green fluro-essen-scents' lora-deep 'neath
a lowism . . . tithing teeth of world—
        hanging on, tagging on, climbing on, giving on,
gaining on, growing on, hearing, my hearing sings for my
seeing to be, one takes the other—when one makes me, one
makes

the one makes me cover the cloudsounding grubber, grabbled
aghast gyrate-shellacker, I jive a joker
for every one three'd, I twice in my headache for a lowcastery,
I could stay in your arms forever but you're
too steady for me, every pull a tiny victory, in our
speckled dustery, limbery trickled-pots, water-pans

dishing out tonight's water-meal, water-home changes
with the thick-lipped clam, whose orange lipstick has
worn off the sides, & she's barnacled mighty to the shelf . . .

I was a shelf you strolled on
my water-green hand, as day goes bye
I was ugly & scary
until the sun came out, me & sun we shake dry to stay
until the very last one has held on

white reefercapped electron—revolving in whatskin
with illcolored coverings . . . yeah, so I take another step

       * * * *

what revolves in cinema smegma

why is it
someone wants to change it
when there is something beautiful

       * * * *

in an alley outside this window
the ghost of last night's dinner pulls up a seat
I can see him eating what I ate last night—
the bricks in this room are only painted on and I wonder
what's really holding the walls up—below me there is a glass ceiling
where I can see paintings of photos hanging on painted walls—
the painting they put in this room is of a rip, there is a painting of a rip
framed in my room and hanging on the bricks, which are painted
the color of the glue between the bricks—at yet another moonrise
inside my mortar walls, I sit, stretched at a standstill

       * * * *

A man tapes an interview with no one
where his voice is the only question
and the music pulls up a chair
d.j. bartender materializes
so what'll it be?

Halo punctures memory sac
flow of image from a reading girl
angry at a madman unsure
if her hormones are up to the task
of hanging with his

Sudden flash of white heat
third eye in the forehead
where white light is liquid lash
at temporary public man
in despair of blank tape

I look up from this writing
the solo interviewer has switched his seat
wonder if he's been switching
back & forth as I've been writing this
how simultaneous

How two events can occupy the same perimeter
what a cycle of generational origins
loss of clarity the further removed
one gets from the original—*grits*
or homefries?

* * * *

what is the correct spot in my house
to sit for inspiration?
throw a blanket on a roar
the city under fear

* * * *

yeah ... so I take another step

* * * *

Into the recklessness
Into the mess
Flat ground caresser
Into you Sun
Can I walk you home
Carry your books
Give you a call
After I know you
Of course
Could I take your orange into mine
And lay at the blue of your restless pounding
My everyday follower
Aren't you tired
Of tracing my every step?
Take a break from me
Sun
Go on
I don't need my shadow all the time
Don't get me wrong
I'd still like to see you, but
You don't have to work so hard
All the time
You make me feel
Guilty and I
Can only bring you what I am
A little something to shine on
When the going gets wild

* * * *

got caught under a spider
big as my hand
embracing the sky
my face under its belly
webs as tall as me
intact
until I stole
one breath

*   *   *   *

prehensile concentration jumps inside the moving mouth

*   *   *   *

we hold each
with each look
a full exchange beyond fluids
we walk out
across our look
for one eyekiss

and this knows direction
this walk through each other
and we dip
with direction and there
we plant our eyes on each other
with a kiss so deep

we see tips of toes
landing on foreign soil
made familiar
by the wander of hands
the walk of direction
drenched by arrival

*   *   *   *

mom's hair is rugged, long and black
sitting in front of me, I see just her forehead
and part of her nose, she travels with her son
for 20 hours on a plane, and her son
with 3-year-old hands, I see just his hands
over the seat, searching through mom's
black forest of hair, and we're all tired on the plane
and over my seat, I see, his hands, his tiny precise fingers
combing, then running, then getting lost in mom's hair,
then holding, then streaming, then twirling, and then hair again,
and then searching, then mommy, then bridges, then hair,
then brushing, then castles, then butterflies, and then twirling again,
then windmills, then climbing, then combing, then brushing, then
waterfalls, then leaping, then hiding, then fingers, then starfish,
then sliding down, then brushing up, then combing, then letting go,
and then islands, and horsies, and holding, and hair, and then
holding, then letting go, then holding, then letting go, and then sleep,
and hair, and sleep, and hair, and sleep, and sleep, and then sleep

                    *   *   *   *

            how patient she is
            to watch me so bad
            or did I write 'want so bad'
            I am king of misdirection, as I need a bad to be
            or so she says when I can't see—and I say
            offit-hum to this kind of night
            one of machinery and dust

                    *   *   *   *

what think has colors unimaginable

has shapes for what is

as I am

passage passenger

tail height — mighty on the mouth

to not see what you see

but what you think you see

for the first time to see something

for the next time

    *   *   *   *

I don't like sitting in the middle
I feel isolated from what's really happening
I'm shut off from the real deal!

    *   *   *   *

"Will all the in-fed children
        please identify themselves—even if
        they know it? Will all lambs in-flight kindly
        rear-down the membrane? From the back, will the
        free-range vegetarians on line for the Vegetarian Liver Paté
        please preserve yourselves for our goldcard members?"

"Sausage Happy ... will the
        page I'm at in my life kindly
        release its goo—for my continue to
        happen in! I'm in suppose for the tenth time in two years
        and I've already released the child-feeding
        to all the monsoons at my de-poseable gripper."

"Will all un-tied infants with salaries higher than diapy yet
    unable to control they bladder ... oh, I'm sorry ... that's
    UNITED infants with an aversion to stigmatic alcoholia
    basking in global warming ... oh, forgive me ... will all shiny people
    unaccustommed to crabbaholy shaving yet prepared for dully ravioli
    rotination—seated higher than first class yet no lower than working class ...
    kindly please immediately take your stations promptly
    by climbing GO! over all who have achieved
    before y ... oh, excuse me ... our flight not yet please wait we call."

*   *   *   *

Fancy in his double-breasted Chauncey
The captain appears
Frenzied inna fit of pansy!

*   *   *   *

THE BLUE-COLLARED BOOBIES ARE IN FULL MIGRATION
THEY'VE LEFT TH' WIVES AT HOME
THEIR CACKLE'S A CALL
TO ALCO-HIJINKS APLENTY, AS YA SEE...
THIY'RRR TRAVEL'N PACKS EN ERE NOISY
SKUFFARDS AJANGLIN' THE CRACKS A'TWEEN THEY CHEEKS, ISSIT
PLENTUM O'PLOONEY, THAT THERE...A CACKLIN' A SEAHEN DITTY —
AMAZE TAROO, THAT THEY STILLED BE ALLA 'PLUT' CATTERS
EN SHAT A RACE FAT!...HMMMPF! HIDES CAN'T AMORE 'N
2 PLEATS THICK! "2 MORE! OI WANT 2 MORE, LASSLE!"

BOYS CLUB FOR MEN, TO ACT LIKE BOYS
WE NEED A MAN'S CLUB...NONE A'THIS DECORUM & DOES IT...!

*   *   *   *

{inchard skullabout rasting ginner
                              backed by ballabout crammed acrinnt}
        {excuser, busybody blousth' boyes away
                    froomth'aisle shella nieds fura passage}

{tuvo walk against the walk
                    if ia see against tho sea is mia wall}
                    {a placed one? or is invention just
                              mia handle pullin' through the gash}

    {against against, is—my walled-day eigher?
                    safe? (ler was safen true), ore iissit ta-blur daflicked}
{a well ov friction...thissen, that I clim't at e'vory
                              dine to doet ad'all?}

        *   *   *   *

    Whew . . . I sat in the sun too long.
    Spongy and low, my body soaked
    with heat. Globes golden, all travolta
    jiminy, I gotta jazzy lift in me!

        *   *   *   *

how a word travels page-ness—cross
your east with an easy disciple or twelve rooted,
in an ocean where staked across its width
is my name as a southern cross covering the expanse
of what I'd never outgrow—if I can't stand tall enough
to be my own shadow, how can I follow the star in front—
whose bait is laced with bittersweet melancholy traced
back to my stance, my posture, heavy
supporting world's . . . wait, fleeting bivalve
in my Achille's moment, I would've
done it, you know . . . I would!

the line between days is a curve before me
a string fading along this wing I have
orange nocturne blue somnamblia
I get reckless when I skip you by

where am I in this heaving spirit, where am I
in the falling odyssey that throws itself
before me, continually . . . I am a spleck
indifferent to the fall, to the gaining orbit
felled by trunks imagined, long lost gotters . . . who is a *gotter*
in this age, who goes and *gets* it—
who rightfully claims a drunken cheer on that boat,
the blue-cloaked dairymen raise their haunched lips
to greet bony skullthrones,
charts of light make their way across
my eyelashes' impermanence, the slow demise
of a farewell wink—where am I in this caravan
bellyful rotten-mouthing by a cracked vision, where was follow
when need painted its curtain across avenue Me,
what do I do in this newfound oblivia, between the restspots
of my lips the roar deletes & my ears are waxed—was this
a fleeting dynamo caught to end expectedly?
or was this a moment above my skull,
to see what I'm all about?

       *   *   *   *

I've been told the sun shines to reveal
the energies of old circuses — in the skeletal remains of
petrified candy cotton fossils, a roller coaster
holds the memory of a universe,
yellow-blue desire charting screams for
flying-high disastros, ribbon marrow twirling childhood,
algae grange & ganged up banners, torn like
so much fleshlip loose-hung to comb the bald sky.

I hear the sun laughs when bringing out
the past—when shining on the rusted cavalry, circlery, merrily,
gone woody to the psycho-shack, splintered muzzle
onna baby's butt, in every ray is a web—
old sun's reminder of what she's yet to catch.

Old sun shows more than she wants to
so bright penetrating, old sun
never sees—just shows.

* * * *

Audrey has flat feet
bumpy motors propel Audrey
across the world

* * * *

In the break, a peninsula
A hitchiker, a thumb
A stand, with two legs on four hands
A stretch, a stick
To be like the color who wants to be mixed

Wailing neuter, shaving echo
Light focuses on my steps, I stay
Unbalanced, cruising in my speed

A kilo, an excess
A metronome sunset, a measure of island
A knife across, the watered screaming
A mosquito bite on my thumb, flaring
At every opportunity

This is the knuckle
This is the ring not fitting
This is the skin, the size too wrong

This is blind reception, the starvant eyehole
Mother Machinacea, molding little mouth-mind
This is the fork, scratched
Across the feather, fork boned
Against mold, scrap heap, this is

Skeletal size as I exist it
Seeing to the sight given / Not born
Misguided tracks
Clock anti-gone / Roar anti-found
This is the tooth hung, the
Stolen mouth around the neck, the shipwrecked skunkhour
Stenched in paradismos sailing, this is the caved-out nostril
The father carved out of my grip
Into sound, this is the warning
Come to life, the borrowed line to step once, to remind once-ing
At every chance, I'm given chance-ing, politely
Pierced, I sliver along, a squared brass, a ring unfitted

*   *   *   *

this is beauty from my part of the world
this is how I look, when I look
this is how I don't use a mirror, this is how
I don't see a picture, this is how I
don't be a thing, this is what I am
when I'm not looking at you
when I don't look at you
you are the most beauty I've seen,
you are to me what I am
to you when you
don't see, I am
the most beauty

*   *   *   *

*   *   *   *

*   *   *   *

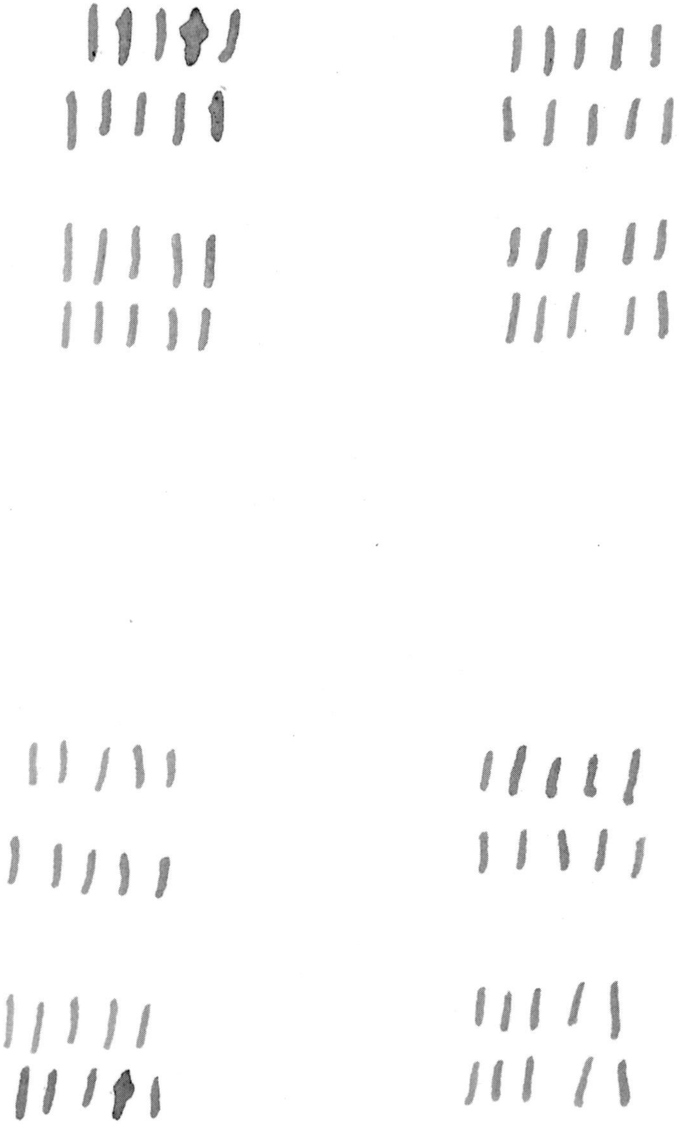

LIMINAL SKIN

A TEXT IN FOUR MOVEMENTS

quiet the garden—becoming sound

quiet the image—becoming sound

quiet the talking—becoming sound

quiet the opposite—coming sound

quiet the ribbon—becoming sound

the air does not believe but sound believes

what does not believe—sound believes

the vox does not belong but box belongs

what does not belong—vox belongs

the age does not behave but falling fades

what does not behave—age behaves

the cloud will never clap but thunder traps

what does not trap—thunder traps

shout the trapped vocalic

shout the giant vowel

shout the echo, shout the wave

shout the mounted growl, shout becoming sound

mute thunder, raining down

out the beginning—coming sound
out the false—becoming sound
out the heathen—coming sound
tether the temperate—blessed sound
out the gale—becoming sound
the mixed implicit—blessed sound

mute thunder, raining down this giant day

voxness, voxism, vo-ism, vosatic, vomadic, vo-ad, voist

vonning, vo-ped, voling out, vayered, the vapid vimistics

visiting vownd, vomiliar, vessel, vickering visionistic visage

of voxed, vale, vapid, vested, vent, of vo-ced, throated,

lie-ed, ryar, byar, flier, tried, my'ed, hoaxed,

coax, boast, yost, most, vessered, blessered,

lessered, tressered, jessered, yessered, noerr'd,

yes'd, no'd, yes'd, no'd, yes'd, no'd until no, until no, until

how come this breeze sounds like me
when I look to the East

how come this same note changes
when I turn to the West

how come the ending is easy
when I face where I've been

how come this home changes notes
when I open this mouth

how can the obsolete surface
be mystery's need

how is the unneed for clarity
the impossible need

what is If and all its patterns
when and family matters

how come anti-clarity becomes catcher
when the unknowing catcher never caught knowing

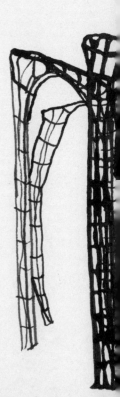

how does the unsentence know to be read
for the audience that never shows up

when did the boy magazine become
the picture not the boy

how come when I look for what I need
what I don't becomes my mirror

what is direction's intention when fabrication
is all I see

how does the obvious error
become the never seen

how come a step is always followed
by the man without beginnings grabbing for the insect that isn't there

how does the giantness of thingness
become the mis-translated beginning

how come time starts to speak
when I turn to the North

when sound travels
in its life
lyric's rhythmic
so erotic a rose is

obsolete
at which point
it is
addressed when

traveled what is
bound to expect is what
the world
waits for

when sound
travels
is
its life

a thorn?
obsolete
when pressed
by love?

but I love
being near you
and how
do you like what you know

what I thought was
knowing
I found
our sound traveled

realistic
resistic
resistant sentence
looks like

static anti-
lyric
what I thought
what was

liminal skin
obso-
lete the
man

without beginnings
tells you what
to see you
look

some-
where else
you think
but I

love
being near
you and how
do you

like what
you
kno-
w

maybe to still the nothing
maybe erased
is all we get
maybe ears are all motion
which only gives me
more motion

I wish there was
no movement
no noise

I wish there was no moment
no reminder
no tremor-filled awakening
no freedom awaiting
no reach of nowness
no stellar sky without tides

hands with giant fingers
roam the earth—no longer
the promise of extinction

luscious moon
are you still there
untold by who needs telling
lucky moon
are you mirror or light

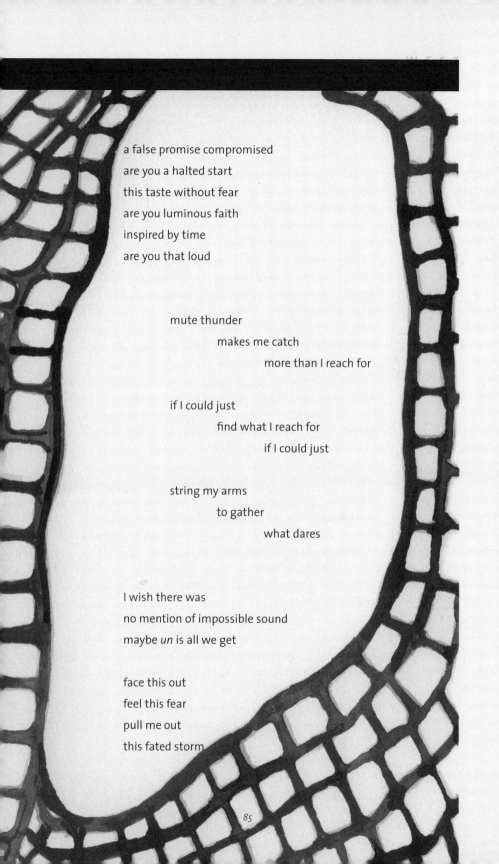

a false promise compromised
are you a halted start
this taste without fear
are you luminous faith
inspired by time
are you that loud

mute thunder
makes me catch
more than I reach for

if I could just
find what I reach for
if I could just

string my arms
to gather
what dares

I wish there was
no mention of impossible sound
maybe *un* is all we get

face this out
feel this fear
pull me out
this fated storm

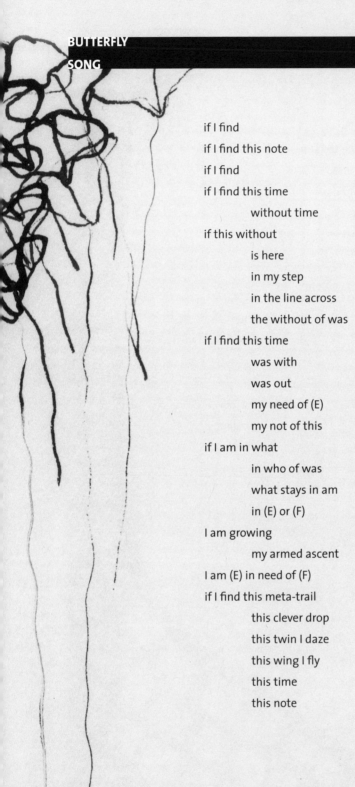

if I find

if I find this note

if I find

if I find this time

    without time

if this without

    is here

    in my step

    in the line across

    the without of was

if I find this time

    was with

    was out

    my need of (E)

    my not of this

if I am in what

    in who of was

    what stays in am

    in (E) or (F)

I am growing

    my armed ascent

I am (E) in need of (F)

if I find this meta-trail

    this clever drop

    this twin I daze

    this wing I fly

    this time

    this note

I once taught my brain to rethink the standing of trees
to unmove the past as a simulacrum for friction

to guard passion with survival
by retraining the remarkable reach of my comfort hook

I once imagined the maze below
as mountains of men sunlit by victory

COME ... climb this hollow shine
allow the molten maggots their millions of features unburdened
by reflection—{*insective selvings who sense surrounding*}

I once impassioned freedom, unpounded by sound
removed by caution, stilled by an ocean of liars
COME ... watch the circular stuffing of concrete clouds

I am inventing the pattern of sound, so my ears may right
the imagined wrong—the air that refuses to budge from sin
the pattern redrawn to fit inside the shape of my stuffed-up ears

> but I tell you ... there is a once
> to this *where* of men
> running with windowless gods
> each breath
> combined
> for the one large breath
> > are you ready
> > to give up your vibration
> > for the one you find at every turn

ür the dirt beneath me, baby
ür seed, ür bass, ür ähhhhhh
öooh, ähhhhhh, ürrrrrrrrr
my clever thyroid cleaner . . .

ür nundo to my mundo
my quiet ürness, my ür to ür ähhhh
the ürday I wished für
waiting for the ërcho of my ähhhhhh . . .

> *choosing the ecstatic wave untold by ü*
> *choosing the ecstatic wave untold by ü*
> *choosing the ecstatic wave untold by ü*

was'n't i, aaaa ü, b'fore with'üt, whn'i, by ü, b'cam
unt'ld, r'told o'reach, out'o'ür . . . mucho mellow choosing?
ür so ocean I fell'in, so bloomin' t' see
whüt ü fa'iled t'be . . . in the my of my-my . . .

ö sailing rectum of punto, baby
ürrrrrrr, m' wish, m'saint's delivery
m'chose, m'clever ending, m'most unnatural
ähhhhhh, öhhhhhh, ürrrrrrrrr' re'ëcho of my ahhhhhhhhh . . .

> need a light . . . ?
> no . . . ?
> n . . . ? mebbe no . . .
> and this, wi'th'ot, b left
> ün'told . . . in the ahhhhhhhhhhhhhhhhhhhhhhhhh
> of the drumsong people

each breath
is each sun

meeting
one direction

what was waiting, are you waiting, what was, waiting was,

what you waited, what, you waited, was what it waits for,

waits, for are you, for what, for waiting, for where you are,

waiting for what you wait for, was, for was, for what it will,

it will, will I want, for what, will I wait, for was

if time
is each sun

is each turn
each breath

I.

there is   really   too much   talk too   really   there is   and this

seeming to   interrupt   is too   you know   what is   after all is

is pretending   seeming to be   really   just   talk   this is   there

finally   the roar   of   after all   too many   you know   people

in my   way too many   you know   really   too much   talk   really

II.

what can find   my vision   sort of   un   realistic you know   expectings

pectations   when I   sort of   never   will have   any   you know

time   to be all   all this   this weight   this many   many layered

skin   I thought   I   thought this was   I was this   I   still   still

reveal   each mirror   each time I   am   a mirror this   this time I

still many times I   I showed up   in reflect   flections   the image   I

I showed up in   up in this   that this was   what it was that   that was I

and I did   I stayed in this   in this image   I was this   many layers   I

was I   this summed up   what it was   I saw   was this   summed

up light   reflected in I   that was what I   was thought this   was that

still   was I that still   each time   each I   one at a time

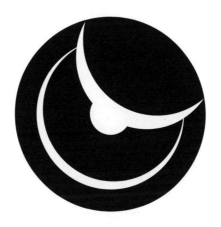

A MOST IMPERFECT START

EROSION

my legs is still attached
and I am still re-tached ... what am I?

my knives are still on fire
and I am not desire ... what am I?

my clouds is without a hat
and I am on my back ... what am I?

my arms is still insect
and I am not respect ... what am I?

> it's not
> that I don't hear you
> it's just
> that what you're saying
> isn't
> what I wanna hear

my trunks is still a furnace
and I am still an ocean ... what am I?

THE MYTH OF A POPULAR DISTANCE
(after Gustave Flaubert)

I

The master of secrets believes in the power
to use story as punctured sky lit by death,
transformed by symbol

> The Sadistic Comet of The Mind
> The Origin of Myth
> The animal who cannot speak like a man
> The shadow of his silence
> Mythos as Mute
> Medusa as Right Blood > Poison
> > Left Blood > Love

Death is connected
to the divine level *mystering* in my work
No one reminds me of these games
and their ultimate creation through enigma—
self's separation is transformation's dawn

> An arrow with its points
> > breaking around me
> A star whose field
> > becomes my story

In the memory of empty catastrophe
in the island of fissures
the hands of the ocean prevent the fisherman
from reaching his shores
Landing on broken answers,
it's possible to imagine—a lace of hands
profoundly pointed
to broken stars

You are my slight detour, sitting next to me
painting the world without fear, skyless and high
a brush for your arms
In the years between my questions
crush my napkin, put it in a cup
hold it and let me drink my empty hands

You are the starting point of my secrets
the end of silent air
Taking an attachment
using it to attack—in a killing life

Using killing as a life, that span of time
a reproducible murder
over the reach of suffering
writing itself over and over

A poet has only one thing to write
and does so for the lifespan of the poet
the one thing is—the writing
Singular and infinite
the poet writes the poet
over and over

II

Dare to reveal
and leave yourself dared—or at least
regretted
Give yourself that which you dare
it leads to decisions at key momentum droppings

To kiss or kill—
dissection of this writing
Castrating poet, brutal alchemist
in search of perfect word

Undaunted by hubbub, unfulfilled by fate—
this connection attempts a shared passage
A breakthrough
for those who want to be broken

My immediate space
is here
between the between
that direct space into dissection

Frankenstonian: my life is not (sic)
consist of event,s (sic)
of thought,s (sic) it is, my fantasia is, (sic)
conversia ultimate

the phantom's pantomime
Epileptic hobo: body contort
creating a symptom to escape life—the unsayable
a symbol for death—a replacement

III

      Oedipal constellation
      Ejaculation of memory
      Images jerked in hallucination
      A thousand symbols
      Erupting into consciousness

The father cures the illness brought on by the father
by doing that which is only allowable by the diseaser, to die
Allowing the son his only remedy—to be with the mother—
The son seeks revenge for giving him bite marks
by constantly dying in front of her
Intersecting castration with self, gazing forward through inward chaos
father makes life real by dying at the hands of materials—
an *artist of life*, realizing his vision

I saw a man who was the confession between
father and brother, a symbolic representation
of lover as dead language
I saw a man who was the anniversary of his birth,
a death candle as research into ambiguous ambiguity
I saw a man who was an external repression,
an installation of transformed relationships, an architecture of privacy
I saw a man linked to a gashed painting torn from sky
knifed onto earth, a reflective participant as a scar of his time
I saw a man who was inviting caressing and touching,
a symbolic cemetary composed of a future
that could not happen, a cementing of hands
inscribed on memory, in flavors I can't pronounce
presented by nowness and thoughts, meant to impress

If this building is a story
it is a height called up from carbon's essence—if I combine these stories
do I read an impulse into connection
do I feel well enough in my *good* architecture for such *privacy*
Rewarded by emotion of morning, soul
is more than I can say

Failing to ignite, what you do
stays on earth, what you see is a series of mistakes
below the failure—ascend to the surface, you'll see eternity
my accomplice to complexity

This is my attempt to relate to the sun
with a series of cuts—I am a visitor
of places without fear, faceless without fear
I am here in your arms
your distance as loud as mine

IV

This is in memory of the disappeared ones
the missing who haven't been
those who once were never, and that
which hasn't yet become

This is a text commemorating that
which hasn't been written, meant
to be invisible as you read it, these very words
are not here, a celebration of memory
the beginning of disappearance

Experience as absence
creation implied, overcoming loss,
not every space occupied,
a mapping of the area, spreading out
over all you can, but—in your own time
Scribbles that slowly fill the page, but each line
its own dimension

This is the voice
that is not yet a voice, a particular negotiation
of closeness with stillness—one of humankind's
oldest structures—the architecture of one's space
All levels of perception, look closer
and toward it,
walk on it—and let yourself, possibly, enter

TEMPEST

everyone will feel better
       hearing what you are saying
              since what you are saying
                     no one told you to say

everyone will feel better
       hearing what you are saying
              since what you are saying
                     no one told you to say

a number of people
       have gathered and stopped
              for whatever it takes
                     to say what you say

a number of people
       have gathered and stopped
              for whatever it takes
                     to say what you say

something is happening
       that hasn't been seen
              making what happens
                     the opposite of seeing

something is happening
       that hasn't been seen
              making what happens
                     the opposite of seeing

saying what there is
in a time like now
means never knowing time
if time can be right

saying what there is
in a time like now
means never knowing time
if time can be right

it is your job
to witness your world
to tell who will listen
so they listen like you

it is your job
to witness your world
to tell who will listen
so they listen like you

we will storm you with words
you will have an entire ocean
we will make you our raindrop
you will have no umbrella
we will teach you our water
you will drown in our words
we will give you an ocean
you will swim in our wash
we will make you our rain
you will have no umbrella
we will water your ocean
you will drown in our words
we will swim in your storm
you will rain in our ocean
we will teach you our water
you will drown in our words

LENS

I am the unknower
stopped—in a fit unplaced
I have arranged for my bare ride
a glacier of fortitude
directionless but simpled—as if
headless in a *having*

The unknown
a mount of stop—unbound
sharpened by crystal my
plummage of ice
hold this lens and see my flight
this trail I leave

> *when one has found their fit*
> *one is forced to reckon with*
> *the space you left to fit in—you step forward*
> *your shadow makes a home*
> *in every new step*
>
> *when one chooses*
> *to become unknown*
> *one stops to arrange choice*
> *I have become the choice itself*

And I ride
on such convenient denial
melting, as I expose
only the part you see

I'll have melted
before you see everything
but you had your chance—
when I offered you the sun
to magnify me with

GYRATIONS OF SARANGEA

we were strangers in the same sentence
I was alien
I may have come here to receive you
but I never wanted to outlast you

unfit muzzle roast lichen murk

how I ember sunk in you
how the clay splays apart
at every minute of you

my shoes are fat thirsty

I was known for battle
a shining of the past
a rock impervious to failure
a scene for seers

abandoned for mystery
my warning
was how I play at your mouth

how I can see
with feelers
that float from my dungeon

I was sent to ride on your back
a ram in the badlands
a prarie on the playfields

A MOST IMPERFECT START

Forever the mighty maze inflicts unchangement
a sly wander from the course unchosen.
If once this could have been what reflected continue
what exposed go, what gave most high staring
its relentless give, which all we wish, was a stay of let.
If once this breath-bomb staggered
to show its true stance; then we, collected breathlessly
by time's stammer, would have found reason for change.

The sportsman aligns himself under the object of his catch
his muscles remember the most accurate procedure.
The sportsman has a child, a home, a wife he loves but not for long,
a drug addiction behind him, a relapse before him, a diamond ring
waiting to be picked up with the initials of his favorite pet
cast in gold across a wealth of gems. He puts all this
out of his mind, his brain blocks this information as it has been
trained to do when his body reacts to the object, 100 feet in the air.

The object was once a cow hit by a tree unspun by machinery,
a breeze through its branches before twine once decided its future.
The tree meets the diamond ring, the breeze unlocked in the sun
meets the house, the wife catches the object, the child runs the field,
the drugs find the twine, the college scholarship makes contact
with the forest, the sportsman uncaught remains staggered
under the object of his catch.

One day a worm approached a caterpillar, lost on the ground
beneath his tree. That conversation became a butterfly
born of misguided hierarchy. There once was a rainstorm of
repetition showering the trees with apprehension. That raindrop
became an ocean for a country of smaller oceans. Once upon
a time there fell an enormous child who tried to brace himself
on whatever he could catch, he would throw something and
lean against it before it would land.

We each have our function-machines set for body salvation
or emotion-bearers, each of us, in what is laid
for most imperfect starts, most unpounceable hearts.
We are each in the guise of body when least aware of body.
I am continually at wander with the reach of everyone around me.
This motion will cut most unexpected matters
and when most unexpected, what survives will be laid bare.

OP THE MISTIC

and yes, a crucible is a teepee is a mountaintop
in microscopic splendor
a nose is an atom is a tear
in my scope of sweethearts
a yes is an ending
unrelied by movement
ours is a window
unmoved by splendor

and yes, an ocean is a sentence is a pillow
is a kiss in cantilevered flight
a drop is a molecule is an ear
in the ducts of what I miss
a listening for a no
fired by a relentless run
a door
ignited by rain

and yes, a temple is a branch is a forest
trapped by steam
a crevice is a hand is a church
in your catch of quasars
a yes is still alive
arrowed by heart
yours is a flicker
pointing at mine

TRUE TO YOU

would you let go
if you knew where
you were going
something, huh...
about falling
and holding on
to what makes you fall
something...
how falling
was the only way
we found each other

Edwin Torres was born in New York City. He is a recepient of fellowships from NYFA, The Foundation For Contemporary Performance Art and The Poetry Fund among others. His books include *The Popedology Of An Ambient Language*, *The All-Union Day Of The Shock Worker*, and *Fractured Humorous*. His CDs include *Oceano Rise*, *Novo* and *Holy Kid*.